796.93
NENT

255

PROPERTY OF SCHOOL
DISTRICT NO. 75

Brace
pur...used with

Title IV-B Funds

1982-83

DATE DUE		
MAR 2 0 1991		
MAR 2 7 1991		
APR 22 '70 7		

HIGHSMITH 45-220

BRACEVILLE SCHOOL LIBRARY

FREESTYLE SKIING

FREESTYLE SKIING

by Jerolyn Nentl

Copyright © 1978 by Crestwood House, Inc. All rights reserved. No part of this book may be reproduced in any form without written permission from the publisher, except for brief passages included in a review. Printed in the United States of America. Reprinted 1978, 1980.

Library of Congress Catalog Card Number: 78-8032

International Standard Book Numbers:
0-913940-90-9 Library Bound
0-89686-011-6

Edited by - Dr. Howard Schroeder
            Prof. in Reading and Language Arts
            Dept. of Elementary Education
            Mankato State University

CIP

Library of Congress
Cataloging in Publication Data

Nentl, Jerolyn Ann.
  Freestyle Skiing.

  (Funseekers)
  SUMMARY: Photographs and text introduce the funda-
mentals of the young sport of freestyle skiing.
  1. Skis and skiing--Juvenile literature.   (1. Skis and skiing) I. Schroeder, Howard. II. Title.
GV854.N42   796.9'3   78-8032
ISBN 0-913940-90-9

Our special thanks goes to the Freestyle Skiers of America and their secre-
tary/treasurer Mary Brooksbank. Most of the photos that illustrate this book
appear through Mary's efforts.

Photo Credits

Freestyle Skiers of America: 3, 5, 7, 8, 10, 12, 14, 16-17, 18, 23, 24A,
        24B, 24C, 24D, 24E, 26A, 26C, 28, 30-31, 32
Focus On Sports: Cover, 20
Marion Post: 12

Scott is ready at the top of the mountain.

The snow is just the way he likes it. The sky is a beautiful blue, the air is crisp, and the sun is warm on his back.

Thousands of people line the ski slope on both sides. Television cameras are aimed at him. Everyone is waiting to watch him "ski the bumps."

Scott is tense and excited. He is anxious for the signal to get going.

He is a professional freestyle skier. Scott is young and an expert on skis.

He skis the moguls. Moguls are the little mounds carved in the snow. They appear after many people have skied down a hill. They are carved by the edges of the skies as the people turn.

Skiing a moguled hill is called "skiing the bumps."

Scott Brooksbank.

Norm Classen and Assoc.

Scott Brooksbank.

Skiing is one of the most popular winter sports. It can be enjoyed by almost anyone. It makes no difference how old a person is.

Freestyle skiing is a new and exciting way to ski. It is for experts only. Experts can be any age. They can be amateurs skiing for fun or professionals skiing for money.

Freestyle skiing is like acrobatics on skis. It is like ballet on skis. It is both frightening and beautiful. It is graceful and aggressive skiing. Freestyle skiers "attack" the slopes! They have positive thoughts about their ability to ski!

It is hard to say exactly what freestyle skiing means. The skier can do whatever comes to mind. The only limits are imagination, athletic ability, and the rules of safety.

Some people call freestyle skiers "hot doggers." Real freestyle skiers do not like to be called that. The freestyle skier is not someone who "bashes" down a ski slope. It is not someone who makes everyone get out of the way. The freestyle skier is an expert skier who moves gracefully and skis with precision.

"Hot dog" makes a person think of someone "showing-off." There was a lot of "hot dogging" when freestyle began. Now the sport has grown up. Most freestyle skiers today are insulted when called "hot doggers."

Mogul skiing is just one part of freestyle skiing. There are many difficult tricks or stunts to do. These are done on the ground and in the air. They are called ballet when done on the ground, but are called aerial acrobatics if they are done in the air after a jump.

There are contests in all three types of freestyle skiing. Both men and women ski in the events. There are about twice as many men as women in freestyle skiing. Men and women compete separately.

Some freestyle skiers were active in other sports first. Some were even champions. Then they started skiing.

Scott Brooksbank was the World Freestyle Skiing Champion in 1972, 1975, and 1976. He had been a college diver on the swim team. Others were gymnasts or surfers, while some were ski racers.

A special camera lens created this interesting shot of an aerial acrobat.

Others began skiing with their families and friends when they were very young. Marion Post is one of these people. She won the most money of all professional men and women freestyle skiers during the 1975-76 season.

Marion has been skiing since she was six years old. She took many ski lessons. Next she went to a freestyle skiing school taught by professionals. Now she is a professional herself. She teaches others how to freestyle ski.

Marion's twin sister, Ellen, is also one of the top women freestyle skiers.

Size does not make champion freestyle skiers. Marion and Ellen are good examples of this. Marion is only five feet one inch tall. Ellen is not even five feet tall. Marion says, "You do with what you got!"

Marion Post.

Freestyle skiing started when good skiers got tired of skiing the slopes the same way every day.

Some days the weather was too bad to ski on the high slopes. At other times the slopes were too crowded. On these days the good skiers went down to the lower "bunny slopes." There they did tricks for each other and the crowds.

No one knows for sure how long skiers have been doing tricks on their skis.

In March, 1971, a ski company sponsored a "hot dog" contest. It was only a mogul event. It was on the steepest and hardest run.

Those who watched thought the skiers were crazy. They went down the run doing anything they wanted to do. The more the crowd roared, the harder and faster and crazier the skiers would ski. This is the reason for calling the early freestyle skiers "hot doggers."

In April, 1971, the first North American Freestyle Championships were held. The ballet and aerial events were included for the first time.

The new kind of skiing, called freestyle, had become a recognized sport!

By the next season crazy "hot dog" skiing was no longer the thing to do. There were too many good skiers. Now the crowd looked for perfection. So did the judges. Wild stunts and falls no longer scored points with anyone. It was no longer "hot dog" skiing. It had really become freestyle skiing.

Many skiers dropped out of the sport at this time. They did not like to be told what they could or couldn't do while skiing. At first anyone could enter a contest. They could do anything they wanted to do to impress the judges. Later there were controls on who could enter, and what skiers could do during the contests.

Safety was one of the reasons controls were put on freestyle skiing. Some falls had injured freestyle skiers. They were afraid their kind of skiing might not be allowed on the slopes at all if there were too many injuries. They did not want this to happen to their sport so they agreed to control it themselves.

BRACEVILLE SCHOOL LIBRARY

Mogul Skiing!

How do you freestyle ski? Let's look at each of the three events separately.

MOGULS

Skiing the bumps or moguls is the way in which freestyle skiing was started. It takes lots of practice to ski a mogul slope like an expert.

Mogul skiing is fast and full of rhythm. It is like a fast dance. How fast a skier can ski through the moguls depends on strength. It also depends on how quickly the skier reacts to turns. Some moguls can be three or four feet high. A good skier can be going 30 to 40 miles per hour through them down the slope.

In contests a skier is allowed to go in the air coming off the moguls. They are not allowed to jump. The winner is not always the fastest skier to the bottom of the hill. The judge also looks at a skier's control. Does the skier hesitate? Was the run skied cleanly? Was the skier in control? There must be control!

BRACEVILLE SCHOOL LIBRARY

AERIALS

The aerials are the most daring of all three events. They are very dangerous. A skier might go 20 to 30 feet in the air. The speed at landing is often faster than that of the mogul skier.

Some aerials are done upside down. These are inverted aerials. Amateurs are not allowed to do them. They are not allowed on regular ski slopes. The inverted aerials are the most dangerous of all and often cause the most injuries.

Each skier does three aerials during a contest. Each of the three must be a different trick.

The tricks have names like:

- side kick or kick-out
- twister
- tip drop
- 360 helicopter
- spread eagle
- front or back somersault
- daffy
- side or tuck somersault.

Aerial skiers are judged on how high and how far they go. They are judged on how well they perform the three tricks. They are also judged on how well they are in control of their landings. A "flight plan" must be filed before the contest. This helps the judges know what tricks are going to be done.

There is a special rhythm to jumping. This makes it beautiful to watch. Jumpers bend their knees, then straighten their body to prepare for the jump. They fly into the air and do their trick. Then they straighten their body to get ready to land. With bent knees the skier hits the ground and carefully straightens to ski off down the slope.

BALLET

Ballet freestyle skiing requires coordination and balance. It requires gracefulness and strength.

Some of the tricks in this event are:

- royal christie
- outrigger
- daffy stand.

The ballet event is skied to music. Skiers can earn extra points if they can ski in time to the music. They can earn more points if they can express the music with their tricks.

Skiers are judged on how well they do their tricks. They are also judged on how smoothly they glide from one trick to the next. How gracefully they move their body also scores points.

Falls are counted against the ballet skier. It is counted against the skier even if only a hand touches the snow. This means the skier is out of control.

A new aspect of the ballet event is pairs skiing. Two people ski the same trick at the same time. Some have skied two people on one pair of skis! Pairs skiing is not yet part of ballet contests.

It might seem men would do best in aerials and women in ballet. This is not true. Scott Brooksbank is a top ballet skier. Marion Post is one of the top aerialists.

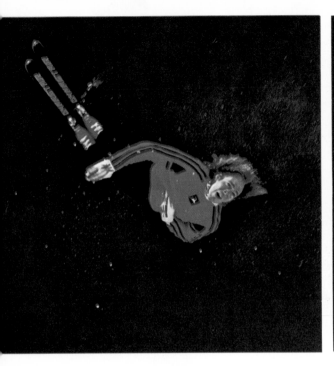

The twister.

The front summersault.

The "tip drop."

Backwards summersault.

"A 360°."

Freestyle skiers must have good equipment. No one could even try to freestyle ski before a few years ago. Ski equipment was not good enough. Skis used for different tricks are not the same length. For example, freestyle skiers use shorter skis for the ballet event than they do for the aerial event.

The skis also have sharper edges and bend easily. This is important when skiing a moguled hill.

Boots are made better. Bindings hold a skier to the skis better than those used in regular skiing. No skier wants the skis to fall off during an aerial. If they do the skier might be seriously hurt or killed.

Watching freestyle skiing is exciting. The experts make it look easy. Only those who know how to downhill ski should try it.

Many skiers just want to try freestyle skiing for fun. They do not want to enter contests or be a professional. This is wise. Freestyle skiing often improves a skier's regular downhill skiing.

Entering contests and becoming a professional leaves little time to do anything else. This can make skiing a real job.

The best way to learn freestyle tricks is to go to a training camp or school. A skier should not try the tricks alone. Camps and schools are advertised in ski magazines. Ski shops and mountain lodges know about them. They are held in the United States, Canada, Europe and South America.

Getting the proper instruction from qualified teachers is the safest and easiest way to learn how to freestyle.

A skier learning to freestyle ski falls often. One

Scott Nelson Photography.

Examples of ballet freestyle skiing.

Susan Huff Photography.

must learn how to fall properly so that the skier will not be afraid of getting hurt. Fear will not keep the freestyler from trying new tricks.

There will always be some falls. Even expert skiers lose their balance sometimes. The expert recovers and stays upright instead of falling. A good sign of an expert is the ability to recover when one's balance has been lost.

A fall should not embarrass someone learning to freestyle ski. It often means trying new things and not being content doing what one already knows how to do.

Falling properly means falling in a relaxed way. The body collapses naturally. This means the knees bend and the body falls backwards to one side. The knees should be kept as close together as possible. One hip should be used as a shock absorber.

A person must be in top physical and mental condition to freestyle ski. Being in good physical condition is a good way to prevent accidents. It will make skiing more enjoyable, too. A skier needs strong legs, thighs and ankles and flexible knees. Good lungs are also necessary to avoid running out of breath.

Getting into top physical condition takes self-discipline. Freestyle skiers even train during the summer to stay in shape. They run, jog, swim and skate. They are often tumblers, divers and surfers. They play tennis. This also helps keep up their strength and builds endurance.

Special summer camps, called "dryland camps," help professionals practice throughout the year. Students can also attend these camps.

Summer time excercise is extremely important to the competitive freestyle skier. This skier uses a trampoline to practice his aerials.

Safety is a very important part in freestyling. There are more risks in freestyle skiing than regular skiing. The speed and daring tricks that are performed in the air make freestyling a most dangerous sport.

Mary R. Brooksbank.

A freestyle skier follows these safety suggestions:

- be in good physical condition
- use proper equipment
- check the equipment often to make sure it is in good condition
- know the slope that is going to be skied
- understand the snow conditions
- understand what could mean trouble at high speeds — and what to do about it
- do not ski fast near obstacles like trees
- do not let anything block your vision of the run
- make sure there are no other skiers in your path
- ski within your ability
- stay in control.

Freestyle skiing is organized on two levels — professional and amateur. Each level has its own set of rules for the contest and judging.

The two levels set safety rules for ski slopes before contests. They make sure skiers are qualified to do aerials. They work to get rid of the "go for broke," "hot dog" image. They also help tell the public about the sport. This is done through contests and television programs.

Amateur contests have been held in the eastern United States since the 1960's. These contests did not start in the Midwest and West until 1973. Amateur freestyle skiing began with young people in the East Coast ski school programs. They were good skiers. They wanted to show how well they could ski.

About 2,000 boys and girls, under 18, ski in amateur contests each year. Many will go on to be professionals. Some will go to work for ski equipment companies.

Canada also has an amateur program. At least one contest with Canada should take place in the near future. There may also be a freestyle skiing event in the Olympic Games by 1984!

Freestyle skiing is a colorful and daring sport. If you are already a skier and think you are good enough, go to a freestyle camp or school and try it. You might end up in the Olympics or on one of the professional ski teams.

Scott Brooksbank.

"GO FOR IT!"